KILLER CREATURES

ALLIGATOR

**DAVID JEFFERIS
AND
TONY ALLAN**

Belitha Press

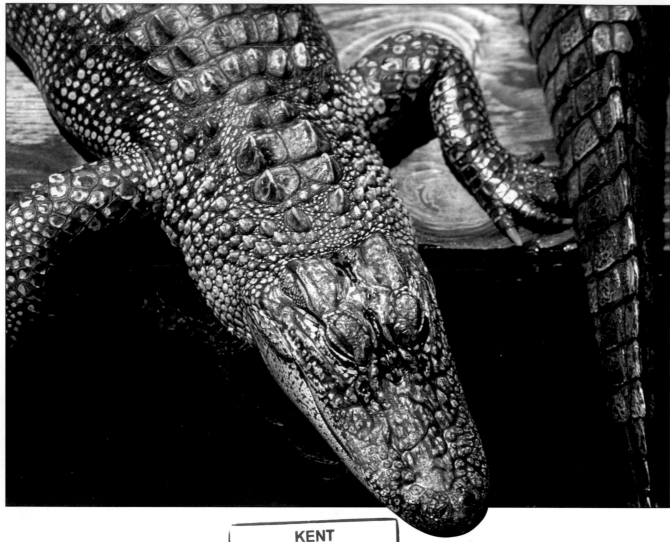

▲ Alligators have thick, leathery skin. Bony lumps stick up along the back for extra protection.

First published in Great Britain in 2001 by
Belitha Press
An imprint of Chrysalis Books plc
64 Brewery Road, London N7 9NT

Paperback edition first published in 2002

Copyright © David Jefferis/Tony Allan 2001

Design and editorial production:
    Alpha Communications
Educational advisor: Julie Stapleton
Picture research: Kay Rowley

ISBN 1 84138 300 7 (hardback)
ISBN 1 84138 379 1 (paperback)

British Library Cataloguing in Publication Data
for this book is available from the British Library.

Printed in Hong Kong

10 9 8 7 6 5 4 3 2 1

Acknowledgements
We wish to thank the following individuals
and organizations for their help and assistance
and for supplying material in their collections:
Alpha Archive, Ardea London Ltd, Jack Bailey,
BBC Natural History Unit, Bruce Coleman
Collection, John Cancalosi, Francois Gohier,
Fuji Film, Nick Gordon, Chris Harvey, Daniel
Heuclin, EA Janes, David Jefferis, Rich Kirchner,
Steven D Miller, NHPA Natural History Photographic
Agency, Andy Rouse, Peter Scoones, Eric Soder,
John Shaw, Lynn Stone, Adrian Warren

Diagrams by Gavin Page

CONTENTS

 LOOK FOR THE ALLIGATOR BOX

Look for the little black alligator in boxes like this.
Here you will find extra alligator facts, stories and
other interesting information!

REPTILES FROM THE PAST

▲ Deinosuchus's skull was almost 2m long. The dog is shown to the same scale.

Alligators of today look much like their ancestors. Millions of years ago, alligators probably lived as they do now, basking by day and hunting by night.

Scientists think that the first alligator-like reptiles lived over 200 million years ago.

    The biggest of these that we know about was the deinosuchus. It grew up to 15m long, more than twice the size of any alligator today.

    Scientists think that many of these early alligators lived at the same time as the dinosaurs.

◄ Deinosuchus could have eaten a dinosaur like this with a snap of its jaws.

▶ Deinosuchus probably looked much like this alligator – but much bigger.

About 65 million years ago, the dinosaurs died out – no one knows exactly why – but some reptiles survived. Today's alligators are little changed from their ancient ancestors.

the ears of an alligator are hidden in thick folds of skin behind its eyes

WHAT IS A REPTILE?

Alligators are reptiles – cold-blooded animals with a backbone and dry, leathery skin, made of horny scales.

A reptile's body temperature matches its surroundings, so a reptile moves back and forth, from hot sun to cool shade, or into the water to stay comfortable. Other reptiles include snakes and turtles, which also lay leathery eggs, like alligators.

THE CROCODILIANS

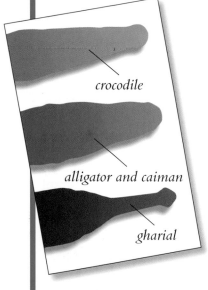

crocodile

alligator and caiman

gharial

Alligators belong to a family of reptiles called the crocodilians. These animals all have huge jaws, short legs, powerful tails and thick, scaly skins.

There are 23 kinds of crocodilian. Most of these are crocodiles, but alligators, gharials and caimans are also in this group. Gharials live in rivers in southern Asia and caimans can be found in Central and South America.

There are two kinds of alligator. American alligators live mostly in Louisiana and Florida, in the southern USA. Chinese alligators live around the Yangtze River, in China.

▲ A crocodile has a head shaped like a thin triangle. A gharial has a thin snout. The head of an alligator is blunt.

► Crocodiles show both sets of teeth when their mouths are shut. Alligators show only their upper teeth.

▲ The spectacled caiman has bony ridges over its eyes.

▲ The gharial's mouth looks like a giant zip fastener.

FAST SWIMMER

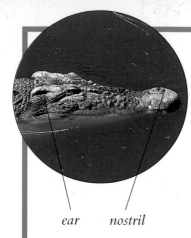

ear   nostril

Alligators spend most of their time in water. Their bodies are perfectly adapted for this, and they can swim faster than you can run.

▲ Alligator nostrils and ears have flaps that shut tight to keep water out.

An alligator's hind feet are partly webbed, like a duck's. This helps the alligator move quickly in water. When the alligator swims fast, its feet are held close to its body.

An alligator's massive tail is very powerful. The tail moves from side-to-side in an S-shape, enabling the alligator to swim at the same speed as a powerboat. Alligators can swim at over 20 km/h for short bursts.

HOLD YOUR BREATH

An alligator can hold its breath under water much longer than a human. Most people can last about 90 seconds. An alligator can hold its breath for about 15 minutes in summer. In winter it can hold its breath for an hour or more.

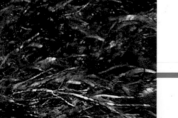

▶ A basking alligator shows off its feet. Only the back feet are fully webbed.

◀ When swimming, alligators use their feet like rudders to help them steer.

When an alligator slows down, it may use its webbed hind feet to tread water. By filling its lungs, the alligator can float high in the water. By breathing out, it can sink just below the surface, with only its eyes and nostrils visible.

ARMOURED HUNTER

Alligators have thick, tough skin. This protects them when they attack their prey.

▲ Weeds give almost perfect camouflage for this alligator, as it looks for prey.

Alligators watch and wait for their prey. Their eyes have cat-like, slit pupils that open like shutters to allow more light in at night. In the back of each eye is a mirror-like layer, which enables the alligator to see very well in the dark. Alligators hunt mostly at night.

 SWEATING OR PANTING?

When humans are hot, they sweat to cool down. Alligators keep their cool another way – like dogs, they use their mouth.

On a hot day, an alligator opens its mouth wide to cool off. The air takes away moisture from the alligator's tongue, and this helps cool the blood as it goes through the mouth. If the day gets hotter, the alligator looks for shade, or cools off in the water.

Alligators eat mostly fish and other water creatures. But an alligator may also attack an animal near the water's edge, such as a snake, a rat, or even a small deer.

After stalking the animal silently, the alligator dives, and swims towards it. Then the alligator jumps out on to the bank, seizes the prey with its huge jaws, and drags it back to the water. When the prey has drowned, the alligator can rip it apart and feed.

▶ An alligator's tough skin protects it against almost anything except human weapons. Thick lumps on the back give extra protection.

▲ Over a short distance, alligators can move fast enough to catch many animals.

lumps on back

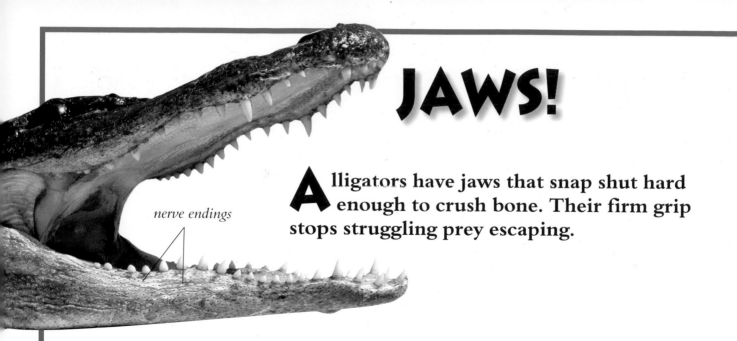

JAWS!

Alligators have jaws that snap shut hard enough to crush bone. Their firm grip stops struggling prey escaping.

nerve endings

▲ These tiny dots around the jaws are nerve endings. They let an alligator feel prey moving in nearby water.

▼ Strong tape can keep the jaws shut. Here a tourist holds a young alligator safely.

Surprisingly, the muscles that open an alligator's mouth are quite weak. People who work on alligator farms say they can hold the jaws shut without much trouble.

It's a different matter when an alligator's jaws snap shut – these muscles are super-strong, and even the biggest prey is unlikely to escape.

DOWN IN THE MOUTH

An alligator's mouth is made to protect it against struggling prey. The skin inside the upper mouth is very hard to protect the alligator's brain if an animal kicks.

At the back of the alligator's mouth there is a flap of skin that can close to block off the windpipe. This lets the alligator battle with prey underwater without drowning.

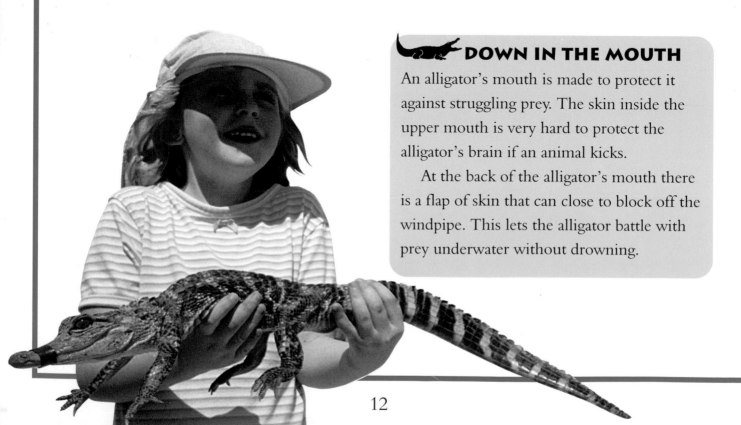

An alligator's sharp teeth are made for ripping and tearing prey. Alligators don't chew their food – they swallow small animals in one piece, while bigger creatures are ripped apart and swallowed in chunks.

New teeth grow as old teeth wear out. An alligator may go through 50 sets in its lifetime.

▲ Alligators may catch food under water, but they eat it above the surface.

► Alligators swallow stones and pebbles to help grind up the food in their stomachs.

MAKING A NEST

▲ Alligator eggs are thick and leathery.

▼ An American alligator opens its mouth to call a mate.

Alligators mate during spring. But it is the females that make nests for the eggs, and later care for their young.

After mating, a female alligator goes off to find a quiet, marshy area. Then she makes a nest. First, she builds a mound of grass, leaves and sticks, pushing the materials together with her back feet.

The alligator crawls over the mound, to pack it down, then digs a hole in the top. She lays her eggs in the hole, about an egg a minute. After half an hour there may be 30 to 40 eggs in a pile. She covers them with wet leaves and mud.

◄ A female alligator takes several days to make a nest. She usually returns to the same nest each year, but the old nest may need repairs before she lays her eggs.

GRUNTS AND HISSES

Alligators communicate using a variety of sounds, including loud, pig-like grunting noises. In the mating season, males and females may bellow loud enough to make the ground shake!

Other sounds include various hissing noises, to threaten other animals or to show distress. Alligators also slap the water hard with their heads, a sound that travels a long way underwater.

ALLIGATOR BABIES

Alligator eggs hatch out about nine weeks after they are laid. Baby alligators stay close to their mother for protection.

When the eggs are ready to hatch, the mother alligator clears the leaves and mud from the nest.

Once the baby alligator (called a hatchling) is out of the egg, the mother may carry it to the water. A hatchling usually weighs about 60g and measures about 20 cm long.

▲ Raccoons like to eat young alligators. So do otters, garfish, owls and snakes.

▲ A young alligator learns to stalk prey in some reeds.

Mother and babies communicate by grunting to each other. The mother sounds rather like a pig, while the hatchlings make squeaks and hissing sounds.

Even though the mother cares for the hatchlings, only about half survive – they make an easy meal for many other creatures.

 A mother alligator carries a baby safely on her head.

READY TO HUNT

Young alligators learn their hunting skills quickly. They have razor-sharp teeth, and start by snapping at flies, minnows, or water beetles – in fact, anything that moves.

As the babies grow, they hunt bigger prey, such as frogs, toads and fish. After a year, young alligators are about 70 cm long, and eat prey such as catfish, water rats and baby birds.

ALLIGATOR HOLES

Alligators spend most of their time in water. They are famous for digging resting holes at the bottom of swamps, lakes and streams.

If there is a drought an alligator hole may be visited by other animals. Fish, birds and other alligators come to share what may be the only water in the area. If the hole dries out, the alligators may have to walk across dry land to find more water.

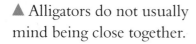

▲ Alligators do not usually mind being close together.

 DON'T FALL OUT!

Birds such as herons and ibis nest in trees and bushes overhanging alligator infested waters. In their nests, the baby birds are protected from hungry animals, such as raccoons and snakes. If these creatures go in the water to try and reach a nest, there is a chance that an alligator will eat them.

But if a chick falls out of a nest, an alligator is usually waiting to snap up a tasty snack.

Alligators are not normally aggressive towards each other, but an alligator hole may get too full for comfort.

In one dry season, over 200 alligators were packed into a single hole. The biggest alligators solved the problem by killing some of the small ones.

▲ An alligator rests in a hole. You can see its track, called a crawl, stretching out behind.

DIGGING A BURROW

Like other reptiles, alligators don't like cold weather. To keep warm in winter, they spend time in special caves, called dens or burrows.

▲ A Chinese alligator at the entrance to its burrow. Alligators usually dig entrance tunnels underwater.

To make a den, an alligator digs a tunnel in the bank of a stream or swamp, using its snout and legs to shovel through the mud. At the end of the tunnel the alligator hollows out a larger area, and that's where it spends much of the winter.

Many alligators stay alone in their dens, although some mothers take their babies inside for their first winter. Alligators become sluggish, but they do not hibernate completely. If a winter day is sunny, an alligator may come out and bask for a while.

striped markings fade as the alligator gets older

▲ This young Chinese alligator may spend its first winter in a burrow with its mother.

WHAT ARE WHITE ALLIGATORS?

Some alligators are white. They are called albinos and are born with no colour in their skin. They are very rare. Few albinos survive long in the wild because they stand out so clearly to predators. Their pale skin does not protect them from the sun's rays, so albinos are easily sunburnt.

ALLIGATOR FARMS

For many years, alligators were hunted for their skin and meat. But so many were killed that alligators had to be protected.

In 1967, alligator hunting in the USA was banned. Today there are millions of alligators living wild there.

Alligators are also kept on farms, where they are bred for their meat, which is low in fat, and for their skins.

Alligator visitor centres are also big business. People love to see these animals close-up, and to learn some interesting facts about them.

▲ Visitors can taste alligator meat at some farms. It tastes a bit like chicken.

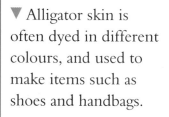

▼ Alligator skin is often dyed in different colours, and used to make items such as shoes and handbags.

▲ Wild alligators are protected in the USA, so this animal can now take a stroll without being shot. Sensible campers keep well clear!

◄ Here visitors can see alligators leaping out of the water to snatch pieces of chicken. Small alligators thrash their tails to help them leap out of the water. Bigger ones use their tails to push hard against the muddy bottom.

HEALTHY DIET

Alligator farmers look after their animals and feed them well. The alligators eat meat, liver, chicken and fish. Vitamins are added to make sure the alligators grow fit and healthy.

ALLIGATORS AT RISK?

Alligators in the USA are protected by law, and are no longer in danger. For the smaller Chinese alligator, it is a different story.

▲ The Chinese alligator is much smaller than its American cousin. It rarely grows more than 2m long.

Alligators used to live in many parts of China. Today, they survive only around the Yangtze River. Rice farmers do not like alligators on their land, and there are very few wild places left for alligators to live in.

There may be only about 1000 Chinese alligators left in the wild. But some special areas have been opened, and here they are starting to breed again.

 LIFE UNDERGROUND

Winters are cool around the Yangtze River, and Chinese alligators spend much of the year living in their burrows. These can have lots of tunnels, with many air holes and several water pools. They are almost like underground villages, so it's no wonder that Chinese farmers do not like alligators digging under their valuable rice crops.

▲ A Chinese alligator guards her nest. It is a big mound, similar to ones made by American alligators (see page 14).

ALLIGATOR FACTS

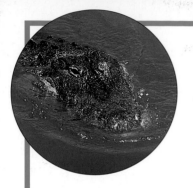

Here are some facts and stories about the world of alligators.

▲ Alligators may live over 60 years. This one is eight years old.

Largest alligator

The largest alligator on record was killed in Louisiana, US, in 1890. It measured 5.6m long.

Oldest alligator

The longest-lived alligator on record died in Adelaide Zoo, Australia, in 1978. It was 66 years old.

Hot eggs

Eggs hatch as males or females depending on the temperature at which they are kept.

If the temperature is above 33.5°C, more males hatch. Below 32°C, there are more females.

Between these two temperatures, males and females are born in equal numbers. No one knows why this happens.

Speedy runner

An adult alligator can run for a short while at nearly 18 km/h. It normally only does this when chasing prey.

Bigger and bigger

Newly-hatched alligators are 19 to 25 cm long. They grow at about 30 cm a year for five years. They carry on growing all their lives, though at a much slower rate.

◄ At visitor centres, staff point out lots of interesting facts. The animals are well looked after.

▲ An alligator holds its front legs to the sides when swimming.

Toothless ones

An alligator grows new teeth to replace ones that fall out, but as it gets older, teeth do stop growing. When it is over 50 years old, it has few teeth left. In the wild, this makes catching prey difficult, so most old alligators starve to death.

Hard belly

Chinese alligators have lumps on their bellies as well as their backs. They are not killed for their skins (unlike American alligators, which have smooth bellies). Instead, Chinese alligators are killed for meat, and parts of their bodies are used for medicines.

Fresh or salty water?

Alligators live in fresh water, while crocodiles can live in salty water. They have special glands to take the salt out of their bodies.

Growing up

Young alligators go around in groups, called pods, until they are eight to ten years old. The only real danger to adult alligators is from humans.

Drowned in their burrows

Chinese alligators spend much of the year in burrows. In 1987, many were drowned when they were trapped by the Yangtze River when it flooded.

Dissolving bones

The digestive juices in an alligator's stomach are strong enough to dissolve a prey's bones, as well as its soft, fleshy parts.

Food for winter

In summer, an alligator stores fat in its tail and body, ready for the winter.

Crushing jaws

Try to imagine a 400-kg weight hitting your little finger. That's about the same force that an adult alligator uses when its jaws snap together on its prey.

ALLIGATOR WORDS

◄ An alligator's slit pupil (see page 10)

Here are some technical terms used in this book.

albino
An animal that is born without any skin colouring. An albino looks white.

basking
To lie in the sun and soak up its warmth. Reptiles do this every morning, to warm up their bodies after the cool night.

burrow
The home an alligator makes for winter. It digs a tunnel from the water, then makes an underground resting chamber.

caiman
A reptile that looks like a cross between a crocodile and an alligator. Caimans live in Central and South America.

camouflage
Colours and patterns used by various animals to help them blend into their surroundings.

crawl
The name for a trail made by an alligator. The crawl is made mostly as a result of the alligator's tail dragging along the ground.

cold-blooded
An animal that cannot warm or cool itself. Its temperature matches its surroundings, so it moves in and out of the sun or into water to stay comfortable. Reptiles normally move quickly only when they are warm – they slow down when the temperature drops.

crocodilian
A number of reptile species that look quite similar. There are 23 species of crocodilian, two of which are alligators, the American and Chinese.

deinosuchus
A huge reptile that grew up to 15m long. It is thought to have lived 200 million years ago.

alligator hole
An area cleared in a lake or stream bed as a resting place.

gharial
A crocodilian with thin jaws, named after an Indian word for a jar with a narrow spout.

hatch
The moment when a baby alligator (a hatchling) is born, when it comes out of the egg.

hibernate
To go to sleep for the winter. Alligators slow down, but do not sleep all winter. On a sunny winter day, an alligator may come out to bask.

predator
An animal that hunts others for food. The alligator is the best predator in its habitat.

prey
An animal that is hunted by another animal for food.

pupil
The opening in the centre of an eye. Humans have round pupils but alligators have slit pupils, like those of a cat. In dim light and at night, pupils open wider, so they can let in more light.

reptiles
A large group of cold-blooded animals that includes snakes, turtles, lizards and the crocodilians. The young of most reptiles hatch from eggs with leathery shells.

▲ Deinosuchus may have looked like this. Scientists have only found a skull, but they can make a good guess as to the size and shape of its body.

scales
The horny plates that make up an alligator's skin.

species
A group of living things that can breed among themselves, and have young that can also do the same.

stalk
To creep silently. An alligator will stalk its prey so that the animal does not know that the hunter is nearby.

◀ An alligator warms up as it basks in the morning sun.

ALLIGATOR PROJECTS

Making an alligator file, with photographs, notes and sketches, will help you find out more about these amazing creatures.

◀ Catching the 'snap' of an alligator's jaws can be a problem. They close so quickly that often all you see is a blur.

▲ A simple camera can give good results if you are careful.

The best place to see an alligator is at a visitor centre. There are quite a few of these, especially in Florida, home of the American alligator, and they make a terrific day out.

Collect your facts in an alligator file – take some photographs and make sketches. Look for alligator stories, to give your file a 'newsy' look.

▶ Label your photos to show points of interest.

the underside of an alligator is a creamy colour

KEEPING THE EGGS WARM

Alligators lay eggs in a mound of vegetation to keep them warm. By day the sun's heat warms the eggs. At night, the mound is like a blanket, protecting the eggs from the cold.

This experiment shows how the covering material keeps the cold away. You can use pre-packed tissue paper that looks rather like a pile of grass.

1 You need two plates, two thermometers and tissue paper – ordinary paper will do. You can make mini-eggs out of coloured plasticine.

2 Place the thermometers and eggs on the plates. If you don't have two of everything, do the experiment one plate at a time.

3 Check the thermometers show the same temperature, then place the tissue paper carefully on one plate.

4 Clear two shelves from the household refrigerator (ask an adult first), then put the plates on them. Leave for about 30 minutes.

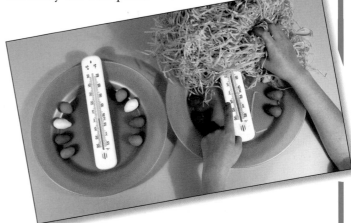

5 Take the plates out of the refrigerator, and check which set of eggs is warmest. It should be the eggs protected under the tissue blanket.

INDEX